Piano Variations

AARON COPLAND

© 1997 Al Hirschfeld. Art Reproduced by Special Arrangement with Hirschfeld's Exclusive Representative, The Margo Feiden Galleries Ltd., New York.

BOOSEY & HAWKES
AN IMAGEM COMPANY

DISTRIBUTED BY

HAL•LEONARD®
CORPORATION
7777 W. BLUEMOUND RD. P.O. BOX 13819 MILWAUKEE, WI 53213

The metronomic markings are to be taken only as approximate indications of correct tempi.

TO GERALD SYKES

PIANO VARIATIONS

AARON COPLAND
(1930)

*) ◇ = press down silently

4

6

not too fast, well articulated

Più largamente ancora ($\bullet$ = 58)

r.h. simile

l.h. simile

Sust Ped.

r.h.

l.h.